GOTTA LOVE IT

A Humorous Play About Rural Life

BY

KATHLEEN MORRIS

Rouge Publishing

OTHER BOOKS BY KATHLEEN MORRIS

<u>Deep Bay Series</u>
Deep Bay Vengeance
Deep Bay Relic
Deep Bay Legacy (Coming 2014)
<u>Blood War Series</u>
The Prion Attachment
Blood Purge (Coming 2014)
<u>Short Inspirations Series</u>
Size Seven Shorts
Short End Of The Stick
Shortcut To Alaska
<u>Short Stories</u>
Along The Way - 12 Short Stories You Can
Read Along The Way
<u>Plays</u>
Time Will Tell - An Easter Play
Even Me - A Christmas Play For Your
Sunday School
All I Need Is Love - A Play For Teens
Lost And Found - A Children's Christmas
Play
Gotta Love It - A Humorous Play About
Rural Life

How - To Books
How To Make Eye Catching Ebook Covers Easily

Available on Amazon.com

Table of Contents

A NOTE FROM THE AUTHOR

Gotta Love It is an AWARD WINNING PLAY of 2001. Originally performed by *Dancing Sky Theatre*. Winner of *The Saskatchewan Rural Writing Contest* in 2001, it is a play about life in rural Saskatchewan. I crafted it after moments in my life, living on the farm. I've learned to laugh instead of cry in situations beyond my control, and I hope that you, my friends, can do the same. Life is far too short to stress over the small insignificant things. May a giggle help you through, and a tear be seldom shed. May you find the peace that you seek and dance with the wind as you brave life's good and bad experiences. I dedicate this play and all the fun that went with it, to you dear readers/performers/friends. Always remember, blessings are often found in the most unusual places. *God Bless!*

CHARACTERS

Bonnie:

She is a young wife who moved with her husband from the city to the country. She is a city girl and is used to finer things in life.

Mom:

She is Bonnie's mother and has always lived in the city. She is high strung and fussy.

Frank:

He is Bonnie's husband. He is a young man in his mid-twenties, carefree and docile. He has a sense of humour and could appear to some as dopey.

Buddy:

He is Frank's friend. He laughs a lot and has a jolly disposition. He is a little dopey.

SCENE ONE

The kitchen of Bonnie and Frank's new farm house. They just moved in a few weeks ago. It was Frank's grandparents home that they inherited, but it's old and decrepit. The kitchen table stands center stage with two chairs positioned at either end. A counter with a wash-basin on top, sits at the right of the stage to represent a kitchen counter and sink. It would be helpful to use a real kitchen counter and faucet if possible. A full coffee pot is on top of the counter as well as two cups, a dishcloth and apron. Two rooms are also visible beside the kitchen table. Anything else that will make a stage look like a kitchen may be used as well but is not necessary

AT RISE OF CURTAIN

Bonnie comes into the kitchen looking discouraged. She puts her apron on and grabs a cloth and starts washing the table. Suddenly she hears a knock at the door, looks at her watch, and throws the cloth on the counter. She wipes her hands on her apron and straightens it…then tries to put on her visiting smile and opens the door.

Bonnie:
Oh hi mom, welcome to our lovely new dive. (*She is being sarcastic when she says the word lovely. She holds onto the door handle with one hand and the other hand is raised to show her mother her home*)

(*This is the first time that Bonnie's mother has been to see her new home since they moved in*)

Mom:
(*She looks around with a smile*) Oh Bonnie...It can't be that bad. (*Her smile turns*

into a frown as she continues to look around)
Oh DEAR! (*She shakes her head*)

(*Mom is still looking around while she pulls out a chair to sit down, Bonnie sits down as well*)

Bonnie:
(*Pouting*) Oh dear is right mom. Just guess what I found in the cold-room this morning. (*She cringes*)

Mom:
(*Curious but anticipating something bad*) What?

Bonnie:
Maggots...EEEEEEW (*She squeezes her face up with disgust, closes her eyes, and shakes her head furiously*)

Mom:
EEEEW! (*She says this at the same time as Bonnie and squeezes her face up with disgust, closing her eyes and shaking her head as well*)

Bonnie:

Yuck!...(*Cringing and upset*) Let's have some coffee. (*Trying to change the subject*)

(*Mom shakes her head in agreement but has a disgusted look on her face as she tries to get her mind off of the maggots. Bonnie gets up and pours the coffee in both cups and brings them to the table and sits back down. While Bonnie is pouring the coffee, Mom begins to talk again*)

Mom:

(*Shaking her head in disgust*) Oh my poor baby! Why did that man have to drag you all the way out here? You're not a farm girl. (*She says this with anger*)

Bonnie:

It was his grandpa's farm...What could I say? (*She sips her coffee sheepishly*)

Mom:

(*Looking frustrated*) I know...but good grief...MAGGOTS? (*Starts to sip her coffee*)

Bonnie:

You think that's bad...I fainted when I saw the toilet. I really did mom. (*She says this with a little too much emotion*)

Mom:

(*She says this as if it's the worst thing in the world*) Let me guess...It's green.

Bonnie:

(*Still emotional*) Try...there's no plumbing!

Mom:

(*Chokes on coffee*) What? (*Mom's mouth is hung open*)

Bonnie:

(*Crying*) Mom...IT'S A BUCKET IN A TIN CAN...I couldn't believe it either! (*She's almost yelling*)

(*Mom is shocked. She brings her hands to her face and shakes her head back and forth in horror*)

Mom:

OH NO!!! (*She moans, disgusted*)

Bonnie:

And get this...Frank expects ME to carry the bucket to the outhouse when it gets full. (*Starts crying when she speaks*) Can you imagine?

Mom:

(*Now Mom's really mad*) Oh, for goodness sake!...Well you just tell that man that he's not getting away with this...Not if I can help it!

Bonnie:

(*Pulls a Kleenex from her pocket and wipes her nose*) Mom don't...Frank will be upset.

Mom:

(*Furious*) FRANK WILL BE UPSET?! What about you? You're upset! I'm upset!

Bonnie:

(*Trying to calm down so her mother will calm down*) I know...but just stay out of it...PLEASE MOM!

Mom:

(*She holds her hands up in frustration as if to say that she'll stop*) ALL RIGHT, ALL RIGHT... But don't come crying to me when you get ringworm, hepatitis, or something from that toilet.

Bonnie:

(*Calmly*) Honey pail.

Mom:

(*Snappy*) What?

Bonnie:

Frank calls the toilet a honey pail.

(*Mom screws up her face in disgust*)

Mom:

Oh, now that's just plain *sick.*

Bonnie:

(*Says this quickly to change the subject*) More coffee?

Mom:

(*Calmer*) Actually (She looks around) I just need some water to thin it a bit.

(*Mom gets up right away looking for the tap*)

Bonnie:

Over there. (*She points*)

(Bonnie looks down at her coffee, jiggles it, and sits)

Mom:

(*Screams*) WHAT IS THIS?...IT'S ORANGE! (*She dumps the coffee out*)

Bonnie:

(*Looks really sorry*) I'm sorry Mom... I forgot to tell you that the water....

Mom:

(*She interrupts her*) What's wrong with the water? (*She leans against the sink*)

Bonnie:

Frank says it's got iron in it... But I don't think it should be so orange.

Mom:

Ya think? Bonnie, what's wrong with your head?… How could you let him talk you into this?

Bonnie:

(*She shrugs like a child and looks down at the floor*) I could get you more coffee.

Mom:

Forget it! You drive me nuts! (*She sets her empty cup on the counter and goes back to sit down*) Do you at least have hot water?

Bonnie:

(*Sheepishly*) Well...kind of.

Mom:

What does kind of mean? (*She rolls her eyes and shakes her head*)

Bonnie:

(*Cowardly*) Well...I think there's something wrong with it. I took a bath this morning and there was only enough hot water to fill a quarter of the tub.

Mom:

(*Fuming*) Well did Frank take a look at it?

Bonnie:

Not yet.

Mom:

(*Eyes rolling*) Figures...Well, did you at least get your bath?

Bonnie:

Well I tried to...but I couldn't wash my hair. The soap sort of clumped together and curdled on top of the rusty water like soup... It didn't look too good.

Mom:

(*Looks disappointed*) Well I guess. (*Meant as a way to rub it in*)

(*Suddenly a mouse runs across the floor*)

Bonnie:

(*Screams*) A MOUSE!..A MOUSE!...A MOUSE!...LOOK! (*Bonnie stands, points, and shrieks*)

Mom:

(*Screams*)
WHERE?...WHERE?...WHERE? (*Stands, jumps, grabs a broom and stands on her chair. Bonnie grabs a broom, stands on her chair, and starts batting at the mouse. Both women are frantic; screaming and pointing at the mouse*)

Bonnie:

(*Panicking*) OVER THERE!...OVER THERE!

(*Mom attempts to hit at the mouse, as does Bonnie. They continue to scream when Frank and his friend come in the door*)

(*Enter Frank and Buddy*)

Frank:

(*Smiling, thinking they are smart*) Well, isn't this a sight for sore eyes. (*Frank and Buddy laugh loudly at the two women and point at them in an unkind manner*)

Buddy:

I can't believe it! (*Laughs some more*)

(*Bonnie gives them both a "shut up" face*)

Frank:

(*Acting like a big shot in front of his friend*) Let me guess...you saw mouse.

Mom:

(*Frantic and bothered, she starts to yell at Frank and let's all their house problems consume her*) YES WE SAW A MOUSE!...AND I SAW YOUR WATER,

AND I HEARD ABOUT THE MAGGOTS...AND AND AND...THE HONEY PAIL!

(*Bonnie's mouth hangs open in shock, as mom drops her broom and shakes her fists in anger and frustration*)

Frank:
(*She gives Frank a dirty look*) Frank DON'T!

Mom:
(*Frantic*) What? What? (*Sobbing and crying she looks at Bonnie*) OH MY POOR BABY! (*She stretches out her arms to Bonnie*)

Bonnie:
(*Glances over to Frank and gives him another dirty look...then looks at mom with sorry eyes*) Mom it's okay, really.

Mom:
What could be okay about this? (*She holds her arms out with palms open*)

Frank:

(*Goes over to Bonnie and helps her down*) Peace...and quiet? Hey sweetheart?

(*Bonnie smiles at Frank*)

Buddy:

And the cow smell... Right Frank? (*He shakes his head to agree with himself and smiles a great big smile*)

(*Mom's mouth hangs open in disgust and Bonnie chuckles with her hand covering her mouth*)

Frank:

(*Looks sideways at buddy*) That too...and and...peace and quiet... Did I say that already?

Buddy:

Totally! (*Over-shakes his head to agree*)

Frank:

Well, anyway, Bonnie's going to make a great farmer's wife. Aren't you dear?

(*Bonnie shakes her head to agree with him*)

Mom:

(*Angry*) Oh no she is not! Tell him Bonnie… TELL HIM!

Bonnie:

Well...It *is* beautiful.

Mom:

(*Still angry and can't believe her ears. She yells*) WHAT?...WHAT? I gotta get out of here. I can't believe it, my daughter's gone nuts. (*Buddy goes over to mom and attempts to help her down. She pushes him away, gets down by herself, and exits the stage*)

Buddy:

I better get going to… Catch ya latter dude. (*He exits*)

(*Frank raises his arm up to say goodbye to Buddy. Bonnie and Frank remain alone in the middle of the kitchen and Bonnie grabs onto his hands as they hold each other*)

Frank:

Bonnie, your mother might think we're crazy, but there's just something about this place that gets to me. I don't know what it is. I guess you just...*gotta love it.* (*He lets out a big sigh of satisfaction as he looks around their new home*)

Bonnie:

I know what you mean.

(*They both exit*)

THE END

ABOUT THE AUTHOR

Award-winning author Kathleen Morris has written numerous articles, poetry, and short stories published in various Saskatchewan newspapers. Her poem *Refuge* is published in a book anthology titled *A Golden Morning*. She has written many plays and skits including her play titled *Gotta Love It*, winner of Dancing Sky Theatre's rural writing contest in 2001 where it was also performed by the theatre troupe in Meacham, Saskatchewan.

Deep Bay Vengeance is Kathleen's first novel followed by its sequel *Deep Bay Relic*. She also writes non-fiction inspirational books about funny stories from her own life. Her latest novel is called *The Prion*

Attachment, first book in the *Blood War Trilogy.* When she's not writing, she enjoys spending time with her husband Barry and their three grown children at her home in Saskatchewan, Canada. For more on Kathleen Morris please check out her Amazon Author page at Amazon.com

OTHER BOOKS BY KATHLEEN MORRIS

Deep Bay Series
Deep Bay Vengeance
Deep Bay Relic
Deep Bay Legacy (Coming 2014)
Blood War Series
The Prion Attachment
Blood Purge (Coming 2014)
Short Inspirations Series
Size Seven Shorts
Short End Of The Stick
Shortcut To Alaska
Short Stories
Along The Way - 12 Short Stories You Can
Read Along The Way
Plays
Time Will Tell - An Easter Play
Even Me - A Christmas Play For Your
Sunday School
All I Need Is Love - A Play For Teens
Lost And Found - A Children's Christmas
Play
Gotta Love It - A Humorous Play About
Rural Life

How - To Books
How To Make Eye Catching Ebook Covers Easily

Available on Amazon.com

www.ingramcontent.com/pod-product-compliance
Lightning Source LLC
LaVergne TN
LVHW051819080426
835513LV00017B/2014